THE WORLD LEADERS AND HOMOSEXUALITY LEGALISATION

THE SECRET BEHIND
(Volume one -1)

THE WORLD LEADERS AND HOMOSEXUALITY LEGALISATION

THE SECRET BEHIND
(Volume one -1)

Maxwell Kobina Acquah
(YEFULKAY)

TATE PUBLISHING
AND ENTERPRISES, LLC

DEDICATION

I whole heartedly dedicate this book to all followers of JESUS CHRIST who is „The Way, The Truth and The Life' - JOHN 14:6 – Jesus saith unto him, I am the way, the truth, and the life: no man cometh unto the Father, but by me.

I also dedicate this book to you the reader.

TABLE OF CONTENTS

iii. Jesus Christ – Above All
iv. Salvation

INTRODUCTION / PREFACE

In this world, our main reference law book for living is the ***BIBLE***; all other religions make reference from the Bible with different interpretations. The Bible is not like any ordinary constitutional book that needs amendment, but can be descended in common language for one's understanding. It is the deep thought of God and is God Himself, John 1:1*; **In the beginning was the Word, and the Word was with God, and the Word was God.*** One cannot just interpret with his or her own thinking, it must be spiritually descended.

The issue of human right and freedom of expressions in defence of advocacy of gay and lesbian have been wrongly defined and erroneously handled. Morality is the opposite of immorality so as deviant behaviour is the opposite of standard or rightful behaviour.

People are hiding behind Human Rights and freedom of speech and expressions, and the biblical phrase *,,,that shall not judge''* to promote what is socially deviant in Christian perspective.

Everything that happens on earth has a spiritual basis. There is a spiritual influence on those involved homosexual act. The bible makes it clear that we are not fighting against flesh and blood but against principalities – *„Ephesians 6:12, For we wrestle not against flesh and blood, but against principalities, against powers, against the rulers of the darkness of this world, against spiritual wickedness in high places.'*

Some leaders in the world, organisation, churches and religions have been attacked by those principalities, powers, spiritual wickedness, and rulers of the darkness. Hence out of pressure, lack of proper counselling, and wanting to cling on to political power or positions, they eventually give up and hence implement homosexuality, other sexual immoralities and social deviant rights. Some of these leaders too are the occult leaders themselves or connected to the occult groups and impose with convincing and pleasure things of those deviant vices to lure others to join them.

The most popular bible quotation they use to lure people is *Matthew 7:1 „hat shall not judge'*. What shall not be judge? Is it those in the act or the act itself? People in deviant act are not to be rejected but be judging in the situation they find themselves in order to get a solution. Judging is made with the bible not worldly view, and whoever makes judgement has to check himself or herself first before making judgement, *Matthew 7:2 For with what judgment ye judge, ye shall be judged: and with what measure ye mete, it shall be measured to you again.* We are to judge to find solution to problems in life but not to judge to condemn others. Recognise that the bible says, we have the right to do all things but not all things are rightful before God.

This book attempts to expose the secret behind the legalisation of homosexuality and other social problems.

CHAPTER ONE (1)

SOCIAL AND CULTURAL PRACTICES

Basically, the word **'*social*'** refers to *the interaction or relationship between man (man and woman) and the environment.* This relationship or interactions includes all living and non-living things and its norms and values, culture, beliefs or custom, ethnic affiliation, complexion, region of origin and so on. Culture is the way of life of a particular people living in a particular community; this life includes the way of dressing, eating habit, language, way of worship, marriage ceremony, festival celebration, naming ceremony and so on.

There is no society without law and order, then that society would be land of total injustice, and all kinds of immoralities. Social and cultural practices are governed by law and order of a particular society. One cannot just get up and do what pleases him or her even if it is deviant in the society. The Bible says that we have the right to do all things but not all things are right before the Almighty creator.

1

„1 Corinthians 10:23- All things are lawful for me, but all things are not expedient: all things are lawful for me, but all things edify not.'

In every society, there are different social and cultural practices. Among Africans, there are moral things that exists naturally, the same as the Europeans, Asians, North and South Americans, and Middle East. It differs from community to community within a region.

Every problem or challenges in life can be traced to principles found in the Bible. Every person, regardless of culture, family or ethnic background, religion, education, complexion, country of origin, position or social status, must either follow these principles or experience the consequences of violating them.

Deviant behaviour or immoralities is any behaviour that the society does not accept, some of the examples of deviant behaviours are arm robbery, stealing, prostitution, gossiping, incest, murder or killing, adulteries, fornications, thefts, false witness, and so on. Many examples can be quoted from the Bible.

2

Below are Bible quotes:
Proverbs 6:16 – 19

6:16 These six things doth the LORD hate: yea, seven are an abomination unto him:

6:17 A proud look, a lying tongue, and hands that shed innocent blood,

6:18 An heart that deviseth wicked imaginations, feet that be swift in running to mischief,

6:19 A false witness that speaketh lies, and he that soweth discord among brethren.

Romans 13:13 – 14, 13:13 Let us walk honestly, as in the day; not in rioting and drunkenness, not in chambering and wantonness, not in strife and envying. 14 But put ye on the Lord Jesus Christ, and make not provision for the flesh, to fulfil the lusts thereof.

Revelation 22:15 For without are dogs, and sorcerers, and whoremongers, and murderers, and idolaters, and whosoever loveth and maketh a lie.

Matthew 15:19 For out of the heart proceed evil thoughts, murders, adulteries, fornications, thefts, false witness, blasphemies:

Moralities or standards of living are what are referred to as rightful behaviour or acceptable behaviour. The summary of morality is love. Love produces caring, kindness, sympathy, justice, consideration or forgiveness, and all good things recorded in the Bible.

Human rights are not the right to immoralities or what is not accepted by the majority of the people in the society. It refers to the basic things the law allows for everyone to enjoy in life and must meet the biblical principles (which have been summed up in love, found in JESUS CHRIST) - ***John 14:15 If ye love me, keep my commandments***.

LAWS AND ORDER

Laws are rules and regulations that govern human beings and other living things like birds and many kinds of animals that live in a particular society. The main purpose of the law is to maintain moral fairness to everyone. Without law there would not be the existence of the police, military, immigration, the judiciary or court, leadership role, and traditional courts or chief's palace. Laws exist to control and make sure there is peace and order.

Law and order go in line with social values, cultural values, moral values, religious values, and the likes. Naturally some social and cultural values, religious and custom values exist as laws and do not need to be written before one obeys them. Law and order are parts of God's creation and have existed the first day God created the earth, *John 1:1 – 4; 1In the beginning was the Word, and the Word was with God, and the Word was God. 2 The same was in the beginning with God. 3 All things were made by him; and without him was not any thing made that was made. 4 In him was life; and the life was the light of men.*

John 14:15: If ye love me, keep my commandments.
Joshua 1:8: This book of the law shall not depart out of thy mouth; but thou shalt meditate therein day and night, that thou mayest observe to do according to all that is written therein: for then thou shalt make thy way prosperous, and then thou shalt have good success.

All nations have rules and regulations that govern their activities so as religions also have their rules and regulations that govern them. The rules and

5

regulations are used to judge "situations" and not condemn individuals out right. It is used to criticise wrong doing and find proper or standard solution for it.

All religious beliefs and secular customs or beliefs quote from the Bible to make judgement, even the atheists do so. People quote from the Bible to criticise Bible believers, in comparison to their religious doctrine, customs and traditions, judiciary processes and procedures and constitutional amendment. What is disturbing is the wrong interpretation of the Bible by some people.

It is up hauling or disturbing to hear some world leaders, religious leaders, and other individuals quoting from the Bible with their twisted or ignorant interpretation in support of deviant behaviour. A common example of this quote they make is *"THAT SHALL NOT JUDGE"*. If that's so then the judiciary institutions including the traditional courts and the likes in every part of the world must be dissolved, and make freedom of all things, whether good or bad. Because judiciary makes judgement to send people to prison, and sometimes pronounce death judgement on people to be killed, yet the Bible says - *that shall not judge*

When the Bible says *"THAT SHALL NOT JUDGE" Matthew 7:1 Judge not, that ye be not judged.* Below are the meanings:

1. A person needs to access himself or herself with the Biblical teachings before judging others. Matthew 7:2
2. It is not referring to criticising wrong doing with the Bible to help solve the problem.
3. Do not judge in your own philosophical understanding of the world or about life.
4. Judge situations or social problems to find possible standard solutions to problems.
5. Recognise that the person in a social or situational problem needs help, and you must help him or her to come out of the problem.
6. Do not judge the eternity of the person, but use the Bible to caution the person.
7. Love your neighbour as yourself and see your fellow in a particular problem as yourself and help out.
8. Do not judge outside the Biblical context.
9. You have to be spiritually discerning before making judgement.

7

10. Recognise that God will judge everyone according to his or her deeds one day.
11. Judge righteously - ***Proverbs 31:9 Open thy mouth, judge righteously, and plead the cause of the poor and needy.***

Laws are made to make sure there is peace and order in the society. They are used to help people out of deviant or immoral situation. For example, when someone is sent into prison for wrongful act, it does not mean the person should be maltreated or mishandled but to be counselled and so that he or she would recognised what brought him or her to prison was deviant or immoral and should desist from it. We criticise to help people out of problems but not to put them into doom. So it is wrong for others to quote a biblical principle that they do not understand to defend what is Biblically wrong. Once upon a time every human being was innocent of his or her existence until the man (man and woman) got to know good and bad. Every person is potential to do wrong and also repent of wrong doing, so judgement is used to bring up a person to the realisation of standard of living but not deviant.

All laws including moral law, cultural law, religious law, natural law, traditional law and the likes are subjected to the Bible; the ones that are not found in the Bible are manufactured or man-made laws.

HUMAN RIGHTS

Human rights in some context can be referred to as social rights, because what most people referred to as human rights are just social basic needs. By this, it would be correct to called it social rights, that is the right to have access to enjoy social amenities such as public toilet, hospitals, roads, attend school of choice, public transport, marry a woman or a man you love, build or rent a house and so on.

Human rights or social rights can be defined as the basic things that everyone should have the liberty to enjoy provided the law (probably the bible) allows it. It varies from society to society, and may depend on the cultural, religious, ethnic, traditional, social and moral values of the society. For example, in the Muslim society a man has the right to marry up to a maximum of four; in some tribes or religion a man cannot marry more than one wife but not so in Christian.

Human rights or social rights are governed by law, and one cannot just get up to claim his or her right of something even if that thing is immoral or deviant in a society. What can be considered as human rights in Christian perspective are the rights that the Bible allows them to be enjoyed by people? As has been stated earlier, all organisations or groups of people including the atheist make references from the Bible to criticise life situations or social life, and therefore everything that must be considered „right' must come from the Bible. So anything that is out of Biblical context is deviant or immoral and cannot be considered as right.

The issue of homosexuality which some countries have legalised it by hiding under wrong definition of human right philosophy is wrong. Homosexuality (gay and lesbian) is immoral or deviant behaviour because the Bible against it. The Bible makes it clear as quoted earlier, ''we have right to do all things but not all things are rightful things to do'' that is why even in human institutions or government system there are judiciary service, and moral, cultural and traditional values to provide sanity in the society. If people are advocating for

10

homosexuality as human rights, then arm robbers, conflict planters, thieves and the likes can equally be considered as their human rights and nobody should be criticise or arrested them for any wrong doing. It is much, much disturbing to hear deviant behaviour advocators hiding behind human rights to support what is not biblical.

God from the beginning in the Garden of Eden gave man free will of choice, but with a condition of death. In my book titled "The Downfall of Man is out of WWH'' outlines why there are sufferings in the world and the reasons why some people do what they do. As has been stated already, God gave Adam and Eve the free will of choice, but there was a condition attached to that free will of choice. God gave a condition to Adam and Eve not to eat the fruit of good and evil, for the very day they will eat shall surely die. There is nothing like free without condition, refer from my book titled "There Is A Condition: Recognising The Conditions of Successful Life'' this book explains into detail the reasons why man cannot live without obeying principles.

God's word ,,'The Bible'' did not record that man and man, or woman and woman, or a human being and animal will leave their parents and join as husband and wife. The bible says that a man and a woman will leave their parents and joined together as husband and wife. Homosexual marriage is abnormal, how come a fellow man insert his penis into the dirtiest part (the anus) of another fellow man or a woman use her tongue or finger or object to insert into another fellow woman's vagina or anus. This is not normal; all those who are in homosexual act have psychological, physical, emotional or social, and spiritual problems. They need help to get out of this situation; they need prayers and proper counselling but not to be condemned out right from the society.

THE HUMAN SEXUALITY
Man
Man as a single sex, has the penis as the main sex organ (sexual drive). The penis is the main sex organ that is used for insertion into a woman's vagina during legal sexual intercourse. It is made up of muscles, many blood vessels and spongy tissue which contains numerous spaces. The tip is the

glans, - is covered and protected by loose retractable skin, the foreskin.

Lying on each side of the base of the penis is the testis – two ovoid (egg – shaped). The two balls are in a loose, sack – like skin called the scrotum or scrotal sac. It does not need hot temperature, and responsible for the production of sperms. When it is used in inappropriate way it may be infected.

When it is used to penetrate the anus of a fellow man or even a woman's anus, bacterial and other dangerous organisms will get into it and hence infected.

Woman
The woman as a single sex has the vagina which is the main entrance for the penetration of the penis during legal sexual intercourse. It is a muscular tube which leads from the uterus and opens to the outside. The vagina and urethra opens separately to the outside at the vulva. Two pairs of lip – like flaps, the labia, enclose the vulva and protect the entrance of the vagina. The vagina receives sperm during sexual intercourse. It is also the canal through which a baby passes to the outside during

birth. Just above the urethra is a small, sensitive muscular protrusion, the clitoris which becomes erect during sexual excitement.

Anus: *is the extremity of the alimentary canal, through which the faeces are discharged.* It is meant for discharge of waste materials from the body, the rectum – where faeces are stored is close to the anus.

Faeces - is the waste matter excreted by the bowel, consisting of indigestible cellulose, food which has escaped digestion, bacteria (living and dead) and water. When the anus is penetrated, the tip enlarges, destruction of elastic wall, developing of sore, unusual discharge of smelled fluid, and other infections. **Faeces**– *is the solid waste that comes out of the anus. It comes from material/food that the body cannot use.*

Sexual arousal usually begins in the brain. That is, your brain responds to a sexy thought or image or having a feeling of closeness or affection toward a partner, or the touch of a partner by sending signals to the rest of your body, especially the genital area. For both men and women, one of the major

14

components of physical sexual arousal is increased blood flow to the genital area causing the clitoris to swell and harden in women and the penis to become erect in men. Also, for both women and men, the heart beats faster, blood pressure increases, and breathing becomes more rapid. So in some basic respects, the process of male and female sexual response is quite similar. But because males and females have different reproductive organs we need to look at how sexual arousal affects the genital area separately.

During sexual intercourse, naturally, there is an orgasm; both the man and the woman will release or discharge fluids during the exciting stage. This is not so in man to man sex (penis into anus) or same sex sexual intercourse, the anus will only discharge faeces which are not healthy and results in many complications. The anus of the man acting as the woman destroys and most of the internal organs will also be affected. Likewise in lesbianism; there would be cuts on the walls of the vagina, enlargement of the vulva, destruction of the fallopian tubes, and introduction of bacterial or fungus or dangerous organisms which can cause great damage to the lesbians.

15

There is not a single biological, physical, emotional or psychological, and Christian spiritual benefits of homosexuality practices, the end results are destruction of anus, sickness and diseases, loss of respect, affected by demons, inability to give birth, and premature death.

CHAPTER TWO (2)

THE HUMAN RACE

Human race refers to all people (mankind), considered together as a group. There are different colours, culture and customs, beliefs, social prestige, and marriage and so on, all constitute human race. God created one person Adam and out of Adam is Eve and out of these two opposite sex people there became the human race (continuity of life).Some people argue that if Human Race or mankind began with two parents, then how did it come about the different colours, culture, region, and the likes, refer from my book titled "The Downfall of Man is out of WWH''.

The struggle of man begins at birth because man is in foreign land, the earth. There is no smooth pathway in life; man has to sweat before surviving. The pressure on earth makes man's decision making of choice very difficult. Every individual is struggling to be recognised by the society. Man (man and woman) has become restless, all because of what to eat, wear, where to sleep, who to marry,

17

how to associate with others, and so on. Man is not always satisfied with what he has in possession, he always asks for more.

In childhood stage a child desires to grow faster to avoid parental control and have his own freedom. In adult stage a man desire to be rich and popular. Every individual desire to be somebody in life; these desires are unsatisfactory. The unsatisfactory desires of man have brought about the legalisation of some deviant behaviours or immoralities that are contrary to the Bible. Example of unsatisfactory desires: here is a poor person who sleeps on mats at the marketplace after market activities, he desired to have a small foam mattress to sleep on, when he got it he desired to move out of the market and get single room to sleep in, when he got the house he desire to get a double bed......... he bought a small car, he desired to have four wheel drive....... that's man (man and woman), he never gets satisfied.

When GOD created Adam, He realised that it was not good for man to live alone. He created companion being the animal and birds but these companions did not match or suit man. So God form a suitable companion being Eve out of man.

This is the perfect match; God did not create another fellow man for Adam to marry. So gay and lesbian marriage is abnormal, the Bible does not approve it, and it is demonic. **Genesis 2:18**

2:18 And the LORD God said, It is not good that the man should be alone; I will make him an help meet for him.

2:19 And out of the ground the LORD God formed every beast of the field, and every fowl of the air; and brought them unto Adam to see what he would call them: and whatsoever Adam called every living creature, that was the name thereof.

2:20 And Adam gave names to all cattle, and to the fowl of the air, and to every beast of the field; but for Adam there was not found an help meet for him.

2:21 And the LORD God caused a deep sleep to fall upon Adam, and he slept: and he took one of his ribs, and closed up the flesh instead thereof;

2:22 And the rib, which the LORD God had taken from man, made he a woman, and brought her unto the man.

19

2:23 And Adam said, This is now bone of my bones, and flesh of my flesh: she shall be called Woman, because she was taken out of Man.

2:24 Therefore shall a man leave his father and his mother, and shall cleave unto his wife: and they shall be one flesh.

2:25 And they were both naked, the man and his wife, and were not ashamed.

By the above Bible quotes, God made woman for man and man for woman for continuity, so Homosexuality is not a normal marriage and should not be recognised as part of human race.

THE DESIRE FOR POWER
The desire for political power, religious power, traditional power, spiritual power, and other powers makes people do things that are not really of God. Some leaders are forced to implement some deviant behaviours such as gay and lesbian because of political or some power they are seeking or do not want to lose.

The legalisation of Gay and Lesbian is not really because the Bible says that shall not judge, but because some world leaders do not want to lose power. The perceived powerful nations, some religious leaders, political leaders, organisational leaders, heads of ministries, and other highly recognised officials have agreed to the legalisation of homosexuality because they do not want to lose power. Pressure upon pressure from those in the homosexual (gay and lesbian) act or in support makes some of the leaders irresistible to their demand. They often make reference to „human rights or freedom of speech and associations'.

Everything that happens on earth has a spiritual basis. Most occult groups are behind the success of some world leaders. They provide help to them to win political power or other high positions. Because some world leaders seek help from evil spirits, they are asked to fulfil certain conditions which go contrary to the standard moral life. Some world leaders are the occult leaders themselves and as part of their rituals, implement the homosexuality. The homosexuality practices is from the camp of the devil, and their agents being the occult leaders and some world leaders are making everything possible to frustrate people with economic hardship and political conflict to get them.

PLEASURE AND FAME

It is funny and disturbing to hear people say that there is more pleasure in same sex sexual intercourse (homosexuality) than opposite sex (heterosexual) sexual intercourse.

In physics magnetism, only opposite charges attract, and like poles repel. Meaning positive and negative attract, whilst positive - positive repel, likewise negative – negative repel (that's there is no attraction in like poles) the same in human beings, man and woman naturally attracts, but man – man, or woman – woman do not attract. Homosexuality is not just a mere social deviant problem but a demonic influence. It has a spiritually, physically, psychologically, and emotionally backing, and must be dealt with spiritually, physically, psychologically, and emotionally. If others are saying they take pleasure out of homosexuality then those people have a very big problem and needs spiritual, physical, psychological, and emotional help to get them out of the situation. The Bible says we are not fighting against flesh and blood but against principalities, so those in the act of gay and lesbian have been attacked, *Ephesians 6:12 For we*

22

wrestle not against flesh and blood, but against principalities, against powers, against the rulers of the darkness of this world, against spiritual wickedness in high places.

In each stage of human development there are challenges. At the adolescent stage to the adult stage, a person would wish to be somebody in future. This is where if care is not taken many young people are deceived by these occult groups with their flashy or luxury things. It is common in the entertainment industry; there are so many things that are happening. Sometimes before one can rise up to the top he or she has to seek help from these demonic groups and in doing so are asked to obey certain rules (practice homosexuality) before they receive the help. Many secrets societies (e.g. brotherhood) are the brain behind all the emergence of immoralities in the world. They do so to please their master (the Lucifer); Lucifer does not offer anything better in life, what he can offers is eternal punishment.

Those who are chasing fame are easily lured by Lucifer tricks, he offers them luxury things, makes them win awards, and so on. He tried on Master

JESUS but could not succeed. The Bible says the love of money is the source of all evil; money is good but one must not greedily rush in life to get it. Life is a gradual process and one should not rush in it eagerly to be famous or wealthy.

PRESSURE TO FIND SOLUTION TO LIFE PROBLEMS

It is now common to see advertisement by agents or connectors of marine spirits and other demonic spirits on the internet, radio, TV, newspapers, magazines, and other media sources to convince people to come for solutions to their problems. As I have already stated there is no smooth pathway in life, there are so many obstacles in life and because of that these demonic organisations or groups capitalise on it to convince people to their side.

Pressures in life make some people to deviate from normal life style to deviant life style. Because of hunger, marital problems, academic problems, desire to win political power, spiritual protection, job positions, and many others, people sought to seek help from occult groups. In life nothing is free, everything is attached with conditions, and there are good conditions and bad conditions. In Christ, the conditions are simple principles which have been summarised in LOVE - *Matthew 22:37 – 40; (37 Jesus said unto him, Thou shalt love the Lord thy God with all thy heart, and with all thy soul, and with all thy mind. 38 This is the first and great commandment. 39 And the second is like unto it, Thou shalt love thy neighbour as thyself. 40 On these two commandments hang all the law and the prophets)*. In Lucifer, the conditions are hunger, hatred, killing, and all kinds of immoralities that his connectors are to fulfil.

All occult or demonic organisations offer help to people with conditions of immoralities or deviant behaviours. They ask people who seek help from them to kill or share blood, steal, rape, create conflicts, and at the end reward them with eternal death. They lure people in so many ways, sometimes, they use the Bible with twisted interpretation; associate themselves with Christian church, pretend to show love, and have adopted some basic social moralities common in all societies.

If people will recognise challenges in life as temporal then they can overcome all tricks of the devil. The devil frustrates people who are not easy to convince with life difficulties and intend helping them. The bible makes it clear that life on earth is not easy but if anyone obeys God, the person will have eternal life. We are on probation because of the disobedience to God by our first parents in the Garden of Eden. Life outside the Garden of Eden is not easy; it is hard with frustrations, so Christians have to recognise that to overcome immoralities.

Read more from my book titled ''There Is A Condition: Recognising The Conditions of Successful Life''

CHAPTER THREE (3)

THE POSITION OF THE CHURCH

The Church refers to the body of Christ for which He is the head. And all those who have accepted JESUS CHRIST as their Lord and Saviour belong to His body. ***Ephesians 1:22-23*** says, ***"And hath put all things under his feet, and gave him to be the head over all things to the Church, which is His body, the fullness of him that filleth all in all."***

The church can be classified into two aspects: The Universal and The Local churches.

- The universal refers to all those who have accepted JESUS CHRIST as Lord and Saviour, and this constitute all local churches who apply the body.

1 Corinthians 12:13 - For by one Spirit are we all baptized into one body, whether we be Jews or Gentiles, whether we be bond or free; and have been all made to drink into one Spirit.

27

1Corinthians 10:32 - Give none offence, neither to the Jews, nor to the Gentiles, nor to the church of God;

Ephesians 5:25 - Husbands, love your wives, even as Christ also loved the church, and gave himself for it;

Colossians 1:18 - And he is the head of the body, the church: who is the beginning, the firstborn from the dead; that in all things he might have the pre-eminence.

Ephesians 3:10 - To the intent that now unto the principalities and powers in heavenly places might be known by the church the manifold wisdom of God,

- The Local Church refers to all denominations that have accepted JESUS CHRIST as their Lord and Saviour and apply to His body and lives by the Bible teachings.

Galatians 1:1-2 "Paul, an apostle (not of men, neither by man, but by Jesus Christ, and God the Father, who raised Him from the dead;) And all the brethren which are with me, unto the Churches of Galatia.

Romans 12:5 - So we, being many, are one body in Christ, and every one members one of another.

Matthew 23:8 But be not ye called Rabbi: for one is your Master, even Christ; and all ye are brethren.

JESUS came to die for everyone, meaning He came to make salvation open to all, and everyone who accepts JESUS CHRIST as Lord and Saviour shall have eternal life. *John 3:16 For God so loved the world, that he gave his only begotten Son, that whosoever believeth in him should not perish, but have everlasting life.* All churches or denominations that teach non-biblical doctrines are in error or false church. That church is not really a Christian church but either an ordinary organisation that have their own way of worship or an occult or demonic organisational group with their own evil doctrines.

The local churches can be classified as Orthodox or Catholics, Pentecostals, Charismatics and other. Each of these classes has their own system of administration, way of worship, and how they use

29

the Bible. Within these classes are local denominations, which also have their administrative systems and others.

Some churches and individual pastors or men of God or Apostle or Arch Bishop or cardinal or pope or father and other titles support the homosexuality marriage. They quote from the Bible *"That Shall Not Judge"* saying that who are they to judge if the Bible says so. Are these people trying to say that when some people are behaving deviant or immorally, they are not to be disciplined? Do these clergy or men of God or pastors discipline their children or church members when they do something wrong or not? Then murders should not be disciplined because the murderer has a reason for doing that, so we will not judge. Any other deviants should not be disciplined because you cannot judge why the person behaved that way. Some of the reasons why these men of God or perceived men of God support immoralities including homosexuality are as follows:

1. Some fear that if they do not support, they may be killed by those in the act.

30

2. Political leaders influence on some church leaders lure them to support the immoralities legalisation.
3. Some churches are not really Christian church but only use the Bible in addition to their own demonic books of doctrines to lure people to their camp.
4. Some church leaders or pastors are occult leaders themselves and pretend to be Christian leaders.
5. Some are afraid of speaking the truth because the church membership may reduce and hence affects the church population and finances.
6. Lack of faith in JESUS CHRIST as some religious leaders or church leaders do not really believe in Him.
7. Pressure from the community that the church is located also frustrates some church leaders to state their view of homosexuality clearly.
8. Some also practice the homosexuality.
9. Lack of divine knowledge.

It is about time Christian faithful's rise up to speak out the truth without panicking. ***Proverbs 31:9 Open thy mouth, judge righteously, and plead the cause of the poor and needy.***

Read more from my book titled ''The Church: Is Not What You Think''

MARRIAGE

Marriage is the union between two people (a man and a woman) who have agreed to stay together as husband and wife after having gone through all the marriage rites that the Bible affirms (allows) it. In the Bible, when God formed Adam, He created companions being all kinds of animals and birds, but God realised these creatures were not suitable for Adam. God formed Eve the woman out of Adam when He caused Adam to fall into deep sleep. When God brought the woman to Adam; Adam said *"this is now bone of my bones, and flesh of my flesh"* meaning it was suitable for Adam and hence he was pleased. God did not form another male (man) to be Adam's partner; He formed a perfect match for him.

Genesis 2:18 – 25
2:18 And the LORD God said, It is not good that the man should be alone; I will make him an help meet for him.

2:19 And out of the ground the LORD God formed every beast of the field, and every fowl of the air; and brought them unto Adam to see what he would call them: and whatsoever Adam called every living creature, that was the name thereof.

2:20 And Adam gave names to all cattle, and to the fowl of the air, and to every beast of the field; but for Adam there was not found an help meet for him.

2:21 And the LORD God caused a deep sleep to fall upon Adam, and he slept: and he took one of his ribs, and closed up the flesh instead thereof;

2:22 And the rib, which the LORD God had taken from man, made he a woman, and brought her unto the man.

2:23 And Adam said, This is now bone of my bones, and flesh of my flesh: she shall be called Woman, because she was taken out of Man.

33

2:24 Therefore shall a man leave his father and his mother, and shall cleave unto his wife: and they shall be one flesh.

2:25 And they were both naked, the man and his wife, and were not ashamed.

If man is to marry a fellow man or woman marrying a fellow woman how can there be procreation? The same sex is not meant to marry because GOD did not make it so. God made marriage for life continuity. The homosexuals and their advocators should ask themselves if their parents had not given birth to them would they have come to the world. Marriage is honourable and must not be defiled, all the things in life for man on earth, wife or husband is the most precious gift one enjoys in his or her life time; the rest are vanity, *Ecclesiastes 9:9 Live joyfully with the wife whom thou lovest all the days of the life of thy vanity, which he hath given thee under the sun, all the days of thy vanity: for that is thy portion in this life, and in thy labour which thou takest under the sun.*
In Proverbs 31:10 – 31 explains who a wife is but not who a gay or lesbian partner is.

31:10 Who can find a virtuous woman? for her price is far above rubies.

31:11 The heart of her husband doth safely trust in her, so that he shall have no need of spoil.

31:12 She will do him good and not evil all the days of her life.

31:13 Sheseeketh wool, and flax, and worketh willingly with her hands.

31:14 She is like the merchants' ships; she bringeth her food from afar.

31:15 Sheriseth also while it is yet night, and giveth meat to her household, and a portion to her maidens.

31:16 Sheconsidereth a field, and buyeth it: with the fruit of her hands she planteth a vineyard.

31:17 Shegirdeth her loins with strength, and strengtheneth her arms.

31:18 She perceiveth that her merchandise is good: her candle goeth not out by night.

31:19 Shelayeth her hands to the spindle, and her hands hold the distaff.

31:20 Shestretcheth out her hand to the poor; yea, she reacheth forth her hands to the needy.

31:21 She is not afraid of the snow for her household: for all her household are clothed with scarlet.

31:22 She maketh herself coverings of tapestry; her clothing is silk and purple.

31:23 Her husband is known in the gates, when he sitteth among the elders of the land.

31:24 Shemaketh fine linen, and selleth it; and delivereth girdles unto the merchant.

31:25 Strength and honour are her clothing; and she shall rejoice in time to come.

31:26 Sheopeneth her mouth with wisdom; and in her tongue is the law of kindness.

31:27 Shelooketh well to the ways of her household, and eateth not the bread of idleness.

31:28 Her children arise up, and call her blessed; her husband also, and he praiseth her.

31:29 Many daughters have done virtuously, but thou excellest them all.

31:30 Favour is deceitful, and beauty is vain: but a woman that feareth the LORD, she shall be praised.

31:31 Give her of the fruit of her hands; and let her own works praise her in the gates.

The above bible reading affirms only the union of man and woman, and condemns homosexuality. The proper marriage is the one that the bible affirms, not the one which the bible condemns.

JESUS ON HOMOSEXUALITY

Jesus is the „word' made „flesh' to live among humanity. What is the word, the Bible? The Bible condemns sexual immoralities including adultery, fornication, incest, and others. 1Corinthians 7 is clear on marriage, it states that let every man have his own wife (woman), and let every woman have her own husband (man).

Any Christian organisation that supports homosexuality or sexual immoralities is committing error or is not a true church.

CHAPTER FOUR (4)

THE NEW WORLD ORDER

The strong nations and other world leaders have suggested a solution to do away the sufferings in this world. They came up with a topic „NEW WORLD ORDER', what is the meaning of this topic called *''new world order''*? Does is it mean the whole world will be going to rule by one nation or president? Or are we all going to follow one pattern of living? Are we in the end time? Why all the sufferings and its implications? Is it something said in the Bible and need to come true? What is the main idea behind this theme called NEW WORLD ORDER. Read one of my books titled:

> Eternity Is Just a Step across the Threshold - www.mkacquah.webs.com   or www.facebook.com/mkacquah

The basic meaning of this is, bringing all the nations together and would be rule by one president choice and decisions. The books of Daniel and Revelations gives account to all the things going on. World leaders always come out with so many suggestions to deal with problems in life yet fails because some of them are not believers.

Out of these troubled times, our…objective - a New World Order - can emerge… Today, that new world is struggling to be born, a world quite different from the one we have known… - Former President George Bush September 11, 1990

The phrase, "New World Order" has been widely used since first coined by George Bush in his 1990 speech before a joint session of Congress.

Although quickly adopted as the catch phrase of the 1990s, few people actually agree on what "New World Order" really means. It has been used to describe such diverse contemporary issues as the post-Cold War balance of power, economic interdependence, fragmentation and the rise of nationalism, and technology advancement and integration - basically any issue that appears new and different.

The general feeling is that while elusive, this "New World Order" is likely significant. Since "New World Order" is most frequently used to describe

39

aspects of the post-Cold War international scenario, understanding the true meaning of that phrase is critical to projecting our future strategic environment and prospects for the new millennium. (By Maj. Bart R. Kessler, March 1997, from OldThinkerNews Website).

It is good to seek solutions to problems in life but that should not be in a situation where the Almighty God is not recognised for His mercies and favour. The only solution that man can seek is God's grace, mercy and favour for man to succeed in living an expected life and qualifying him to have eternal life.

HUMAN IDEA NOT BIBLICAL

The new world order sounds like a biblical idea, but most of the suggested ideas are out of biblical context. The Bible does not encourage slavery, conflict planting, racism, discrimination, sexual immoralities, and other unbiblical things. Some of the world leaders do encourage conflict, slavery; sexual immoralities, supply war machines and equipment to rebels (and are referred to as conflict planters).

The world leaders (some of them) or some powerful nations pretend providing aids to poor countries but force them to implement certain behaviours which are biblically deviant. Most of the oil rich nations have been under attack by these perceived powerful nations; they create conflict by using some unknowledgeable citizens in the poor or under developed nations. Most developed nations do not want the other nations to develop and are using all means to keep the nations undeveloped and dictate to them. This is the hidden main agenda of the new world order.

Poor and under develop nations are under pressure to implement homosexuality. This is wickedness, how can somebody from different nation enforce another to do their will. This is slavery, if not slavery why should powerful nations or some powerful world leaders dictate to somebody in his own nation.

Most conflict in Africa and other parts of the world are created by some developed nations; they supply war machines and other equipment to rebels or opposition party to fight against sitting president (a visionary president) if the president is able to resist their will. A nation wants to claim superiority over the other so always they have to bring them down and keep them under their control. The new world order is a sign of the end time. The bible says, at the end time, nations will fight against nations, hunger, homosexuality marriage, incest, increase in knowledge and many others. It is a man's idea to rule the world in his own interest and philosophies. If the new world order supports homosexuality, and other unbiblical philosophies then watch out for the emergence of anti-Christ.

Anti-Christ refers to someone who claims superiority over nations with his own philosophy rather than *JESUS CHRIST* teachings. This person will enforce immoralities and other unbiblical doctrines. Whatever is implemented in your nation or world compare it with the bible, if it is not of biblical context, then it is a man's idea and not from God. Man's idea cannot give you eternal life, but eternal damnation, so be biblically knowledgeable.

EFFORTLESS ATTEMPT

The New World Order would be an effortless attempt to solve problems in the world because the earth would be destroyed one day by God. No man can solve problems in the world with human limited idea that may be outside of biblical context. Only JESUS CHRIST is the solution to problems; this means eternal life is of JESUS only.

Since the bible has prophesied that the world will come to an end, all attempts are effortless. What man should seek are temporary solutions to basic life problems such as sickness and diseases, shelter, food, social amenities, ego, and other basic needs. The idea to find permanent solution to life problems would be effortless. When God banished Adam and his wife Eve from the Garden of Eden, He cursed both of them. *Genesis 3:15 - 23*

3:15 And I will put enmity between thee and the woman, and between thy seed and her seed; it shall bruise thy head, and thou shalt bruise his heel.

3:16 Unto the woman he said, I will greatly multiply thy sorrow and thy conception; in sorrow thou shalt bring forth children; and

43

thy desire shall be to thy husband, and he shall rule over thee.

3:17 And unto Adam he said, Because thou hast hearkened unto the voice of thy wife, and hast eaten of the tree, of which I commanded thee, saying, Thou shalt not eat of it: cursed is the ground for thy sake; in sorrow shalt thou eat of it all the days of thy life;

3:18 Thorns also and thistles shall it bring forth to thee; and thou shalt eat the herb of the field;

3:19 In the sweat of thy face shalt thou eat bread, till thou return unto the ground; for out of it wast thou taken: for dust thou art, and unto dust shalt thou return.

3:20 And Adam called his wife's name Eve; because she was the mother of all living.

3:21 Unto Adam also and to his wife did the LORD God make coats of skins, and clothed them.

3:22 And the LORD God said, Behold, the man is become as one of us, to know good and evil:

and now, lest he put forth his hand, and take also of the tree of life, and eat, and live for ever:

3:23 Therefore the LORD God sent him forth from the garden of Eden, to till the ground from whence he was taken.

The bible makes it clear that man will not have total peace in the world because of disobedient to GOD. Man has to sweat before finding food to eat, a place to sleep, how to cure his sickness and diseases, and all basic life needs. Jesus came to provide salvation to all who would accept Him as Lord and Saviour. We are outside the Garden of Eden and outside the Garden are where there is no peace, and we can only have total peace when we seek the kingdom of God first, *Matthew 6:33 – 34 But seek ye first the kingdom of God, and his righteousness; and all these things shall be added unto you. 34 Take therefore no thought for the morrow: for the morrow shall take thought for the things of itself. Sufficient unto the day is the evil thereof.* Without the recognition of Jesus Christ, whatever a man seek is useless and the reward is eternal death. Jesus has promise that He will come for the righteous to a place where there are no problems but enjoyment.

CHAPTER FIVE (5)

THE PROPHECY

One should not be surprise of all the immoralities going on in this world. The bible says that when the world is coming to an end, there will be economic hardship, civil war, tribal war, and emergence of anti-Christ, sexual immoralities, and the likes. The books of Daniel and Revelation, the bible as a whole gives accounts for the end time signs. If it does not happen then the bible is not authoritative and would be finite. The prophecy must be fulfilled and it's happening, so what believers need to do is holding on to their faith in Christ.

SIGNS OF THE END TIME

In Mark chapter 13, one of JESUS disciples asked Him how the new world (Heaven) would be like, and what would be the signs of the end time. Below is the quote and Jesus answer: *Mark 13:1 - 37*

13:1 And as he went out of the temple, one of his disciples saith unto him, Master, see what manner of stones and what buildings are here!

47

13:2 And Jesus answering said unto him, Seest thou these great buildings? there shall not be left one stone upon another, that shall not be thrown down.

13:3 And as he sat upon the mount of Olives over against the temple, Peter and James and John and Andrew asked him privately,

13:4 Tell us, when shall these things be? and what shall be the sign when all these things shall be fulfilled?

13:5 And Jesus answering them began to say, Take heed lest any man deceive you:

13:6 For many shall come in my name, saying, I am Christ; and shall deceive many.

13:7 And when ye shall hear of wars and rumours of wars, be ye not troubled: for such things must needs be; but the end shall not be yet.

13:8 For nation shall rise against nation, and kingdom against kingdom: and there shall be earthquakes in divers places, and there shall be famines and troubles: these are the beginnings of sorrows.

13:9 But take heed to yourselves: for they shall deliver you up to councils; and in the synagogues ye shall be beaten: and ye shall be brought before rulers and kings for my sake, for a testimony against them.

13:10 And the gospel must first be published among all nations.

13:11 But when they shall lead you, and deliver you up, take no thought beforehand what ye shall speak, neither do ye premeditate: but whatsoever shall be given you in that hour, that speak ye: for it is not ye that speak, but the Holy Ghost.

13:12 Now the brother shall betray the brother to death, and the father the son; and children shall rise up against their parents, and shall cause them to be put to death.

13:13 And ye shall be hated of all men for my name's sake: but he that shall endure unto the end, the same shall be saved.

13:14 But when ye shall see the abomination of desolation, spoken of by Daniel the prophet, standing where it ought not, (let him that readeth understand,) then let them that be in Judaea flee to the mountains:

13:15 And let him that is on the housetop not go down into the house, neither enter therein, to take any thing out of his house:

13:16 And let him that is in the field not turn back again for to take up his garment.

13:17 But woe to them that are with child, and to them that give suck in those days!

13:18 And pray ye that your flight be not in the winter.

13:19 For in those days shall be affliction, such as was not from the beginning of the creation which God created unto this time, neither shall be.

13:20 And except that the Lord had shortened those days, no flesh should be saved: but for the elect's sake, whom he hath chosen, he hath shortened the days.

13:21 And then if any man shall say to you, Lo, here is Christ; or, lo, he is there; believe him not:

13:22 For false Christs and false prophets shall rise, and shall show signs and wonders, to seduce, if it were possible, even the elect.

13:23 But take ye heed: behold, I have foretold you all things.

13:24 But in those days, after that tribulation, the sun shall be darkened, and the moon shall not give her light,

13:25 And the stars of heaven shall fall, and the powers that are in heaven shall be shaken.

13:26 And then shall they see the Son of man coming in the clouds with great power and glory.

13:27 And then shall he send his angels, and shall gather together his elect from the four winds, from the uttermost part of the earth to the uttermost part of heaven.

13:28 Now learn a parable of the fig tree; When her branch is yet tender, and putteth forth leaves, ye know that summer is near:

13:29 So ye in like manner, when ye shall see these things come to pass, know that it is nigh, even at the doors.

13:30 Verily I say unto you, that this generation shall not pass, till all these things be done.

13:31 Heaven and earth shall pass away: but my words shall not pass away.

13:32 But of that day and that hour knoweth no man, no, not the angels which are in heaven, neither the Son, but the Father.

13:33 Take ye heed, watch and pray: for ye know not when the time is.

13:34 For the Son of man is as a man taking a far journey, who left his house, and gave authority to his servants, and to every man his work, and commanded the porter to watch.

13:35 Watch ye therefore: for ye know not when the master of the house cometh, at even, or at midnight, or at the cockcrowing, or in the morning:

13:36 Lest coming suddenly he find you sleeping.

13:37 And what I say unto you I say unto all, Watch.

Below are the breakdowns of the above Bible quote:

i.   Jesus is asked to reveal these signs Mark 13:1-4

ii.   Listings of these signs – wars, and rumours of wars Mark 13:7 – 8;

iii.   persecution of Christians Mark 13:9, John 15:18-21;

iv.   false teachers and an false Christ Mark 13:6,22, 1John 2:18-19

v.   the worldwide spread of the Good News Matthew 24:14 *''And this gospel of the kingdom shall be preached in all the world for a witness unto all nations; and then shall the end come. ''*, Revelation 7:1-10

vi.   the great tribulation Mark 13:14-20

AUTHORITY OF THE BIBLE - *INFALLIBLE, INERRANT, AND IMMUTABLE*

1.   Infallible-cannot fail
2.   Inerrant- without error - ALL of God's word is trustworthy
3.   Immutable- cannot be changed - cannot change
4.   Inspiration and Authority

a.   *Authority* - the power and prerogative belong to God - flow to us from His Word (make sure to get the order correct; we don't want to impose our interpretations of the bible on God and try to fit him into our box...)

b.   *Authority for faith*
     1. Faith as belief - trust put in the Infallible, Inerrant, and Immutable Word of God
     2. Faith as doctrine - taught by the Infallible, Inerrant, and Immutable Word of God
     3. Faith as religion - built upon the Infallible, Inerrant, and Immutable Word of God

c.   *Authority for Practice* - be not mere hearers of the word, but doers...

JESUS CHRIST – ABOVE ALL
Jesus Christ is God in the flesh. He existed before time and creation "John 1:1 – 5" but on God's appointed time he came to earth in human form as the Son of God, born of the Virgin Mary who rejoiced in God her Saviour at the marvellous thing he had done. Jesus did not cease to be God during

his earthly ministry but for us and our salvation, did not use his divine power so that he might offer up himself as the perfect sacrifice for our sin. Jesus suffered in every way as we do - except sin. The pain he experienced on the cross was as real as the two criminals dying beside Him. Jesus came to die as a sinless sacrifice on a cross so that the penalty for sin might be paid for and sinners might gain and victory over death, the curse of sin. Jesus bore our sins in His body on the cross. God made Him who knew no sin to be sin for us so that in Him we might become the righteousness of God. When Jesus died, He experienced death fully as a man. On the cross He was rejected by the Father since, although He did not sin, He had become sin for us, bearing the penalty for our sin on the cross. After three days, He rose again. He then appeared to many of His disciples giving them various proofs of who He was. Jesus then ascended into heaven and will come again in bodily form to judge the living and the dead. Jesus is the King of kings, the Lord of lords and the Prince of Peace. One day, "every knee will bow and every tongue confess that Jesus Christ is Lord to the glory of God the Father" Philippians 2:10.

Bible references:
Jesus Christ the Messiah Acts 17:3; Son of God Mark 14:61; Jesus God/Man John 1:1, Hebrews 4:15, Mark 1:41; His pre-existence Isaiah 9:6 – 7, Micah 5:2, Philippians 2:6, Colossians 1:15 – 17, Revelation 1:4,8 etc.

SALVATION

Salvation from the penalty of sin is by grace alone and through faith alone (Ephesians 2:8-10). Good works will not save anyone. No one will get to heaven by his or her good works. Each person must individually come to his senses like the prodigal son "Luke 1511:32", humble himself or herself „before God', repent of sin (have a change of mind from doing things their way to God's way - acknowledge they are sinful and God alone is good), turn from sin and put personal trust in Jesus Christ as the incarnate Son of God and His death as complete payment for all their sin: past, present and future. A person is not saved by baptism, going to Church, taking communion or the Lord's Supper, praying, doing good, giving money to the poor or to the Church or by any other means except this: a person is saved from the penalty for their sin (damnation to eternal hell in the lake of fire) by God's undeserved grace, through faith in Jesus Christ as God in the flesh and in his death as FULL payment for their sin. Jesus said, "Repent and Believe the gospel". (Mark 1:14 - 20). In God's mercy, He does not give the repentant sinner what he deserves – hell "Lake of fire". In God's grace, He gives the repentant sinner what he does not deserve – Heaven "God's Kingdom". When a person is "SAVED" they are forgiven, reconciled with God, made a member of the body of Christ and given eternal life in heaven. Bible references: Galatians 5:7; 2:20 – 21; 5:13; Ephesians 4:1; 2:8 – 10; John 1:12; 3:16 – 17; Acts 13:38 – 39; Romans 3:23; 6:23; 1John 5:1- 5; Eph. 2:8 – 9; Philippians 2:12; Colossians 2:13 – 14; John 14:6.

Eph. 2:8-9; For by grace are ye saved through faith; and that not of yourselves: it is the gift of God: Not of works, lest any man should boast.

Grace Alone!
Titus 3:5-7; Not by works of righteousness which we have done, but according to his mercy he saved us, by the washing of regeneration, and renewing of the Holy Ghost; which he shed on us abundantly

through Jesus Christ our Saviour; that being justified by his grace, we should be made heirs according to the hope of eternal life.

Rom. 11:6;And if by grace, then it is no more of works: otherwise grace is no more grace. But if it be of works, then is it no more grace: otherwise work is no more work.

Faith Alone!

Rom. 3:28 Therefore we conclude that a man is justified by faith without the deeds of the law.

Rom. 4:4-5 Now to him that worketh is the reward not reckoned of grace, but of debt. But to him that worketh not, but believeth on him that justifieth the ungodly, his faith is counted for righteousness.

Christ Alone!

Jn. 14:6 Jesus saith unto him, I am the way, the truth, and the life: no man cometh unto the Father, but by me. (KJV)

Acts 14:12 Neither is there salvation in any other: for there is none other name under heaven given among men, whereby we must be saved.

Jesus Christ did all the work to save us from our sins. This is summed up nicely in what is called the

"Romans Road" ROMANS 3:10 As it is written, There is none righteous, no, not one: ROMANS 3:23 For all have sinned, and come short of the glory of God; (KJV)

ROMANS 5:8, But God commendeth his love toward us, in that, while we were yet sinners, Christ died for us.

ROMANS 6:23, For the wages of sin is death; but the gift of God is eternal life through Jesus Christ our Lord.

ROMANS 8:1a, There is therefore now no condemnation to them which are in Christ Jesus,

ROMANS 10:9 That if thou shalt confess with thy mouth the Lord Jesus, and shalt believe in thine heart that God hath raised him from the dead thou shalt be saved.

ROMANS 10:13 For whosoever shall call upon the name of the Lord shall be saved.

CONCLUSION

Dear lovely friend, I do not intend to condemn anyone but to point out the committing errors in the society. Note that this book is a Bible base doctrine and not just an ordinary reading book. I am always inspired by the Holy Spirit to write to bring to the attention of man what GOD demands from us, Jeremiah 30:2 – thus speaketh Lord God of Israel, saying write thee all the words that I have spoken unto thee in a book.

There are certain things that are beyond human understanding and unexplained, unknown. These are MYSTERIES of JEHOVAH ALMIGHTY GOD "the I AM GOD''. ("To understand God it is not necessary to find the answers to every question that comes into your mind". Stay before God so He can give you understanding through the Holy Spirit of what is important. The word was written by the Holy Ghost and it is spiritually discerned). You cannot understand the Bible with your own human thinking (understanding).

For the LORD giveth wisdom: out of his mouth cometh knowledge and understanding. (PROVERBS 2:6)

Now we have received, not the spirit of the world, but the spirit which is of God; that we might know the things that are freely given to us of God. Which things also we speak, not in the words which man's wisdom teacheth, but which the Holy Ghost teacheth; comparing spiritual things with spiritual. (1Corinthians 2:12- 13)

But seek ye first the kingdom of God, and his righteousness; and all these things shall be added unto you. (MATT. 6:33; LUKE 12:31; PHILIPIANS 4:19; JN. 6:27; ETC)

6 Jesus saith unto him, I am the way, the truth, and the life: no man cometh unto the Father, but by me. 13 And whatsoever ye shall ask in my name, that will I do, that the Father may be glorified in the Son.14, 15 If ye shall ask any thing in my name, I will do it. If ye love me, keep my commandments. (John 14: 6, 13 – 15)

Wherefore God also hath highly exalted him, and given him a name which is above every name: 10 That at the name of Jesus every knee should bow, of things in heaven, and things in earth, and things under the earth; (Philippians 2:9 – 10).
If you are not born again, JESUS is right at your door asking you to open HIM to give you salvation.

If your life is NOT right with Jesus Christ/ YeshuahHaMashiach or do not know HIM then pray the following prayer from the bottom of your heart:
"Dear GOD the Father, Son and the Holy Spirit, I come to YOU in the wonderful and most POWERFUL name above all names, the name of Jesus Christ. I am a Sinner, come into my heart and redeem me with YOUR POWERFUL Blood and wash me from all sin. Please send YOUR Holy Spirit to lead me and teach me in YOUR ways. Please write my name in the „LAMB's Book of Life'. Thank YOU for protecting me with YOUR POWERFUL blood that was shed on the cross of Calvary. This I pray in YOUR wonderful name, the name of Jesus Christ. Amen!"

Find a well Bible believing Church who believes in the JESUS teachings and go.

Please; I believe you have enjoyed this book about homosexuality in relation to Bible teachings. And if so, you will probably want your friends / colleagues to enjoy the same, won't you?

Find a well Bible believing Church and worship with them or you can join The Church Of Pentecost if there is one in your area or town or city or country.

Volume two of this book explains into detail the subject of *THE WORLD LEADERS AND HOMOSEXUALITY LEGALISATION - THE SECRET BEHIND (Volume one)*

Criticisms are welcomed through yefulkay@gmail.com or infoyefulkay@gmail.com

You can also visit www.mkacquah.webs.com or www.facebook.com/mkacquah for more information.

DEFINITION OF SOME BASIC TERMS IN SEX EDUCATION

A

Abstinence: Choosing not to have any kind of sex. Someone who practices sexual abstinence does not run any risk of contracting an STI or having an unwanted pregnancy.

Acute: Not lasting a long time. For example, a cold that lasts only two or three days could be referred to as acute.

Anal sex: When a man puts his penis inside someone's anus. This is also called anal intercourse.

Antibody: A disease-fighting protein in the blood created by the immune system.

Antibiotics: Medicine that kills bacteria and some other germs, but not viruses.

Anus: The small opening ("butt hole") in a person's rear end.

Asymptomatic infection: A state in which the person is infected by a virus or bacteria but does not have any signs or symptoms. A good example of someone with an asymptomatic infection would be a person who has herpes who never shows any signs or symptoms of infection.

B

Bacteria: Bacteria are one kind of microscopic (too small to see) germ. Many types of bacteria can make people sick or cause infections, and can be exposed to some of these when they have unprotected sex. There are medicines called antibiotics that kill bacteria. Some sexually transmitted infections caused by bacteria include chlamydia, gonorrhoea, syphilis and trichomoniasis.

Barrier: Something that stops or blocks things from going past it. Condoms act as a barrier between one person's body fluids and another person's skin. Dental dams (sheets of latex) or plastic wrap can also be used as barriers for oral sex.

Biopsy: Removal of tissue from the body for a diagnosis.

Birth control: A method used to prevent pregnancy; another phrase for contraception.

Birth control pills: One form of contraception. Birth control pills are hormonal pills that a woman can take every day to keep from getting pregnant. Once inside the body the hormones tell the ovaries not to release eggs, so a woman doesn't get pregnant. Birth control pills do not prevent STIs or HIV-- they only prevent pregnancy. Most people simply call it "the pill".

Bisexual: A person who is sexually attracted to both males and females.

Blood borne virus: A kind of germ that lives in blood and can't live outside of the blood stream for very long. Air, heat and chemicals can easily kill this type of germ. There are many blood-borne viruses, including HIV and hepatitis B.

C

Casual contact: Everyday things that we might do with other people. Hugging, holding hands, kissing with a closed mouth, wiping tears, playing games, drinking from the same glasses, eating from the same plate, or borrowing soap or clothes are examples. These are NOT ways someone can get sexually transmitted infections, including HIV, from another person.

Cervical secretions: These fluids come from a woman's cervix and out of the body through the vagina. They are usually a whitish colon. If a woman has HIV or another STI, her cervical secretions can transmit (give) the STI to another person.

Cervix: The lower part of the uterus, with an opening into the vagina.

Chancre: A sore that appears at the place where infection with syphilis takes place. The sore is generally not painful for women; however it can be very painful for men.

Chronic: Happening for a long period of time.

Circumcision: A procedure that removes the foreskin of the penis. While not all males are circumcised, when they are, the procedure is usually done soon after a boy is born.

Clitoris: An organ above the opening of a female's vagina and above the opening of the urethra. It is located where the folds of flesh come to a point in the top front part of a female's pubic area, between the labia. It is a very small, sensitive bump that feels good when it is rubbed or touched. Slang terms: clit.

Coitusinteruptus: Oral, vaginal or anal intercourse that stops before ejaculation inside the receptive partner--also known as "pulling out." It is not effective as a means of preventing pregnancy or the transmission of STIs.

Colposcope: An instrument that uses a special magnifying lens to examine the tissues of the vagina and cervix. An examination using a colposcope (called a colposcopy) may be used to detect any abnormalities on the cervix.

Communicable: Something, like a germ or virus that is spread from one infected person to another.

Conception: The moment that a man's sperm successfully fertilizes a woman's egg. The sperm and egg fuse to form a zygote, which will eventually grow into an embryo and then a fetus.

Condom (male): A cover for a male's penis. It can be made out of thin latex (rubber), polyurethane (soft plastic) or natural membranes (animal skin). Condoms are used to prevent pregnancy and to prevent STIs, although natural membrane condoms do not prevent STIs.

Confidential testing: If you get a confidential test for HIV or another STI, then only you and the healthcare provider who performed the test can see the results. If someone wanted to see the results they would have to get your permission.

Congenital: A condition that occurs at or around the time of birth; a congenital condition may be acquired (as an infection), or may be hereditary. STIs may be acquired at or before birth, but no STI is genetically transmitted.

Contraception: A term for ways to prevent pregnancy. Some types of contraception prevent ovulation (releasing of an egg), fertilization (meeting of egg and sperm), or the implantation of a pre-embryo in the uterus. Some ways are permanent and others let a woman get pregnant when she or her partner stops using them. Birth control pills, spermicide, diaphragms, sterilization and condoms are some examples of contraception. Not all contraception stops people from getting HIV and other STIs. Only latex condoms stop pregnancy and HIV from happening. Abstinence is the only

100 percent method for preventing both STIs and pregnancy.

Cum: Another word for an orgasm or ejaculated semen/sperm.

Culture: A special substance that is used to grow germs. It may also mean the process of taking a specimen from a person and putting it into the special substance. Cultures may be used to diagnose certain STIs, such as chlamydia, herpes, and gonorrhoea.

Cunnilingus: When a person kisses, licks or sucks on a female's genitals. This is one way to have oral sex. People can get STIs this way. If they are doing it to someone who has an STI they can get the germ if infected blood or sexual fluid gets inside their mouth. If someone is doing it to them, they can get infected if blood from the infected person's mouth gets inside their vagina. A moisture barrier such as a dental dam or plastic wrap stops this from happening either way.

D

Deficiency: Something lacking or missing. A person's body that cannot fight germs doesn't have a strong immune system. In other words, they have a deficiency-- not enough germ fighters.

Dental dam: A sheet of latex that can be used to cover the vagina or anus during oral sex in order to prevent body fluids from passing from one person to another and prevent skin-to-skin contact. Use of a dental damn can help reduce the risk of STIs during oral sex.

Diagnose: To tell when a person is infected or sick with a specific disease or illness.

Diaphragm: A form of contraception. A diaphragm is a soft, rubber cup that fits over a woman's cervix to prevent sperm from entering the uterus and prevent pregnancy. It does not stop the male or female from getting STIs from each other.

Dildo: A sex toy that is either in the shape of a penis or another rounded shape. It can be made of plastic or another material and put inside an anus or a vagina. Sharing sex toys like dildos can be risky if they have vaginal fluids, blood, or faeces on them. Sharing sex toys without cleaning them or using a

71

condom can potentially expose a person to STIs. The safest practice is not to use sex toys.

Discharge: When used in talking about STIs, it means a fluid that is sometimes runny, thick, or lumpy. The fluid can come out of the vagina, penis, or anus. A discharge can be a sign of a STI or some other infection.

Douching: Using water or other solution to clean the vagina and cervix. Douching won't prevent the transmission of STIs and can't prevent pregnancy. Douching can even encourage certain infections of the vagina. For most women, douching is unnecessary because the vagina is self-cleaning.

Dysplasia: A change in the size, shape, and organisation of cells. One potential cause of dysplasia of the cervix is human papillomavirus (HPV).

E

Ectopic pregnancy: Pregnancy that happens outside the uterus and usually refers to pregnancy occurring in the fallopian tube. An ectopic pregnancy cannot turn into a normal pregnancy. In some cases, if an egg keeps growing in the fallopian tube, it can damage or burst the tube and cause heavy bleeding that could lead to death. An ectopic pregnancy may be the result of pelvic inflammatory disease (PID).

Egg: A woman's sex cell, stored in the ovaries. A female is born with all the eggs she will ever have--about 1-2 million. The ovary typically pushes out one every month, about two weeks after a woman has her period. An egg can live only two days after this happens if a sperm enters the vagina and finds the egg a woman can become pregnant.

Ejaculation: The act of semen coming out of a male's penis during an orgasm. This can happen during sex, masturbation, or even when he is asleep (wet dream). If a male doesn't ejaculate during sexual contact, there is no physical harm. A male can ejaculate with or without having an orgasm.

Embryo: When a fertilized egg grows to be a certain size and sticks itself to the inside of the uterus, it is called an embryo.

Erection: When a penis gets stiff and hard. This happens because blood flows into it. This might happen because someone is sexually excited, but it can also happen at other times. A hard penis will get soft again after ejaculation or orgasm. It could also get soft before these things happen.

Exposure: Being exposed to a STI means that you were in a situation in which you had a chance to "catch" it. You can be exposed to a STI by having sex with an infected person. It is possible to become exposed to an STI but not infected. You can lower your chance of being exposed to a STI by not having sex or by using a condom correctly and consistently.

F

Fallopian tubes: The tubes that eggs move through to go from the ovaries to the uterus. An egg leaves the ovary and rides along the tube until it gets to the uterus.

Faeces: The solid waste that comes out of the anus. It comes from material/food that the body cannot use.

Fellatio: Oral sex, performed on a man (when a person kisses, licks or sucks on a man's penis).

Female condom: A condom designed to fit inside the vagina. Made out of polyurethane, the female condom consists of a soft pouch that is inserted into the vagina before sexual intercourse to help prevent pregnancy and protect against STIs.

Fertile period: The time of a month during which a woman can become pregnant. It is usually a period of eight days during her menstrual cycle. Up to five days before ovulation (because sperm can live this long inside the body), the day ovulation happens, and two days after (the lifespan of an egg).

Fertilization: The joining of a man's sperm cell and a woman's egg cell. If the fertilized egg gets to the uterus and sticks inside, then pregnancy begins.

Fetus: Eight weeks after fertilization, an embryo grows into a foetus.

Fluid: Any kind of liquid usually used to describe one on the outside or inside of a person's body. Examples of body fluids are: semen, vaginal secretions, saliva, and blood.

Foreskin: Loose skin that covers the tip of the penis on an uncircumcised man. When an erection occurs, the foreskin will pull back.

French kissing: A kiss in which both people open their mouths. One person puts their tongue into the other person's mouth. Most STIs are not passed this way.

Frottage: When two people rub their bodies together so that they feel good for some type of sexual pleasure. Another phrase for it is dry-humping.

G

Gay: Another word for homosexual – specifically men partners.

Gender: (From the World Health Organization) Refers to the socially constructed roles, behaviours, activities, and attributes that a given society considers appropriate for men and women.

76

Genitals: The sex organs on the outside of the body. A female's genitals are her vulva and clitoris. A male's genitals are his penis and testicles.

Glans: Another word that means the tip or head of the penis.

Groin: Another word for the pelvic area on a person.

H

Hereditary: A trait or characteristic that is genetically passed from either the mother or the father to a child. No STI is passed genetically from a parent to their children.

Heterosexual: A person who is attracted to someone of the opposite sex. Males that are attracted to females and females that are attracted to males are called heterosexual.

Homosexual: A person that is sexually attracted to someone of the same sex. Males that are attracted to males and females that are attracted to females are homosexual. Female homosexuals are also referred to as lesbians.

Hormones: Chemicals that a body makes to help other organs do their job.

Hymen: A thin piece of skin that stretches over the opening of the vagina. There is a small opening in it to let blood flow out of the vagina during a period. People used to think that a hymen that wasn't broken meant a girl was a virgin. Now we know that it has a small hole in it that can get stretched more just from running, playing or using tampons. Some girls are even born without a hymen.

I

Immune: To be protected or safe from something. Most people who get chicken pox as children are immune to chicken pox for the rest of their lives. There are vaccines that can make you immune to certain infections, like hepatitis B.

Immune system: A group of cells inside the body that all work together to keep a person healthy by killing germs. These cells can tell the difference between the cells that are part of the body and those things that don't belong inside someone. They defend or protect the body from invaders like viruses, bacteria and other germs. Lymph nodes and white blood cells are two parts of the immune system.

Incubation period: The time period that goes from the first day a person gets an infection until the time he or she starts to show signs or symptoms, if symptoms appear at all. Depending on the infection, this can be as short as a few days or more than 10 years. With some infections, including many STIs, a person may never show any signs or symptoms of disease. Even though an infected person may feel perfectly healthy and show no symptoms, they still can still give the infection to another person.

Infected: Another way to say that someone has "caught" a germ is to say they are infected. If a person is infected with a disease-causing germ there is a certain amount of time (called an incubation period) between the time you get infected and the time that you show signs or symptoms of the disease.

Injecting drug users: People who use needles to put drugs into their bodies, drugs like heroin, cocaine or speed can be injected into a person's veins. Steroids are usually injected into someone's muscles. People who share needles to inject drugs can get HIV or other blood borne infections like hepatitis B. The blood that gets into the needle from one person's body can then get into another person's body when they use the same needle. The risk of catching an STI through needles can be eliminated by either not sharing needles or sterilizing them between uses.

Intercourse: Any type of activity that involves the sharing of body fluids, or the penetration of an orifice (the mouth, vagina, or anus) between two or more people. Sexual intercourse also includes oral sex and anal sex. People can get STIs, including HIV, if they have sexual intercourse without a safe barrier that prevents the fluids from getting from one person to another. Other STIs, like herpes and HPV, can be transmitted during sexual intercourse, even when using a barrier, because these are transmitted through direct skin-to-skin contact.

L

Labia: The inner and outer folds of flesh that cover a female's vagina; sometimes called the "lips" between a female's legs. The outer pair is larger and hair grows on them, while the inner pair is smaller and made of a mucous membrane. These folds of skin help cover and protect the vagina and the urethra.

Lambskin condom: A type of natural membrane condom. These condoms are not recommended for preventing the spread of STIs. Natural membrane condoms have holes called pores in them that are too small to see but are large enough for germs to get through.

Latex: A thin type of rubber. Dental dams and most types of condoms are made of latex. If used correctly and consistently, condoms that are made of latex can prevent pregnancy as well as STIs.

Lesbian: A female who is homosexual (sexually attracted to other women).

Lubricant: A wet and slippery product used during sexual intercourse. Lubricants can be used with condoms, or inside a woman's vagina or a person's anus to make it slippery. This

81

can keep a condom from getting dry and breaking during vaginal or anal sex. There are two kinds of lubricants: water-based and oil-based. A water-based lubricant is best to use with latex condoms because it doesn't make holes in the condom.

Lymph nodes: Round little bumps found under the skin, part of the immune system. Lymph nodes are found in the neck, armpits and groin. They clean the blood by catching and stopping germs and dead cells. One way doctors and nurses sometimes check for an infection is to feel a person's lymph nodes. If the nodes are swollen, then it means the person's immune system is working to kill whatever is infecting the body.

M

Masturbation: Touching a person's sex organs for pleasure. This could be a male rubbing his penis or a female rubbing her clitoris because it feels good. People can do it alone or with another person. Masturbation is not harmful. It does not cause acne or blindness, make people crazy or cause any other awful things to happen. Most people masturbate at some point in their lives.

Menstruation: The periodic discharge of bloody fluid from the uterus occurring at more or less regular intervals during the life of a woman from age of puberty to menopause also called *a period*. During pregnancy, a woman will not menstruate. A missed period is often the first symptom of pregnancy a woman will notice. If a female is sexually active and misses a regular period, she may be pregnant.

Monogamy: Choosing to have sex with only one other person. One way to prevent STIs is to have a mutually monogamous relationship (where both partners agree only to have sex with each other) where both partners have tested negative for STIs.

Mucous membrane: The soft, pink tissue that lines all of the natural openings in the body. The mouth, eyes, nose, throat, vagina, anus and the hole in the penis (the urethra) have these linings. Mucous membranes have small holes in them. If a virus or bacteria that can cause an STI gets on a mucous membrane, then that virus or bacteria can go inside someone's body.

83

N

Natural membrane condom: A condom made from the skins or parts of animals. Natural membrane condoms can help prevent pregnancy, but not STIs. This is because natural membrane condoms have microscopic holes called pores in them. Germs that cause STIs can go through these holes and then inside the body of other people during sex.

O

Oil-based lubricant: A lubricant made from something that has oil in it, like Vaseline, mineral oil and lotions. The oil in oil-based lubricants can eat holes in a latex condom, allowing germs that cause STIs, including HIV, to go through it. To prevent STIs, only use water-based lubricants with latex condoms.

Oral sex: When a person kisses, licks, or sucks another person's genitals to make them feel good. People can get STIs this way if blood or sexual fluids got inside someone's mouth, or if there is contact with a sore from an infection such as herpes or syphilis. Also, STIs can be transmitted if infected blood from someone's mouth gets inside another person's penis, anus, clitoris or vulva. Barriers and latex condoms can be effective in stopping someone from getting infected.

Orgasm: A strong, intense, good feeling that happens in someone's genitals during sex. When a male has an orgasm, he usually ejaculates. For a female, it typically involves spasms that can last for a few seconds or a minute or longer. Someone can have an orgasm just by thinking about sex, while masturbating, or when having sex with another person. Orgasms don't always happen every time someone has sex. Females can get pregnant even if they do not have an orgasm.

Ovaries: The part of a female's reproductive organs that store eggs. After puberty, the ovaries push one egg out each month. Ovaries also make hormones that help the menstrual cycle work. Most females have two ovaries, one on each side of the uterus at the ends of the fallopian tubes.

Ovulation: When an egg is pushed out of the ovary. After ovulation, the egg moves down one of the fallopian tubes toward the uterus. This usually happens about 14 days after a female has her period.

P

Pap test: An exam of a female's cervix. During a Pap test, a healthcare provider scrapes cells from the cervix and then looks at them under a microscope. Cells that look abnormal could be a warning of a cervical infection or cervical cancer, but not always. According to the American Cancer Society, a girl should get her first Pap test by age 21, or within three years of having sex - which ever happens first.

Penis: The male sex organ outside the body between the legs. It is made of soft spongy tissue and blood vessels. The tip of the penis is very sensitive and gives the male pleasure when it is touched.

Period: The time at the end of a female's menstrual cycle when blood comes out of the vagina. This is the blood that would have lined the uterus for a fetus to use to grow if an egg had been fertilized by a sperm. When this doesn't happen, the blood lining the uterus isn't needed and it is released from the body. A period typically lasts between 3-7 days. It is possible for a female to get pregnant while having a period and a girl could get pregnant even before she has her first period.

Plastic wrap: Household plastic wrap can be used as a barrier during oral sex. A piece large enough to cover the vulva, vagina, anus or clitoris can be used as barrier. Plastic wrap does not work as an effective barrier on the penis and should not be used instead of a latex condom.

PMS (Pre-Menstrual Syndrome): Physical pain or emotional difficulties that a woman might have up to two weeks before she has a period. This could be things like cramps, sore breasts, bloating or holding extra water inside the body, or headaches. Sometimes people feel sad, angry or depressed. Not every girl or woman has PMS.

Polyurethane condom: A condom made out of a plastic called polyurethane. Polyurethane condoms are an alternative for people who are allergic to latex.

Pre-seminal fluid: Fluid released from a man's penis before he ejaculates. Most men do not know this happens because they cannot feel it coming out. Pre-seminal fluid can get a woman pregnant and can also transmit STIs, also called *pre-cum*.

Pubic area: The area between the legs in both males and females where the genitals are located. After puberty, this area is covered with pubic hair.

Pulling out: When a man removes his penis from another person's vagina, anus or mouth before he ejaculates also called withdrawal. It does not keep a person from spreading an STI, and it will not keep a woman from getting pregnant.

R

Rape: Forced sexual intercourse. Any person who makes someone have sex with them when they don't want to do it--a husband, friend, date or stranger--makes rape happen. This is against the law. The person who is raped might feel guilty, like they did something wrong, or even ashamed. This is not true. Rape is not about sex, it is about violence. It is important for the person to find someone they trust to talk to about it.

Reproduction: This is the whole process involved in making a baby.

Reproductive organs: The parts of a human body that do things to help make babies. Each part has a different job to do. In a female these parts would be the fallopian tubes, ovaries, uterus, cervix and the vagina. In a male the parts would be the penis, scrotum and testicles.

Rhythm method: A way that some people use to keep from getting pregnant. People try to do this by not having sex on the days that a woman would usually get pregnant. This is usually a few days before, during and after ovulation. Because it's hard to figure out when this happens in each woman, it usually doesn't work very well. It also doesn't stop germs that cause STIs from getting into people's bodies when they do have sex.

Rimming: Contact between the mouth, lips or tongue of one person in or around the anus (butt hole) of another person. It is one kind of oral sex. People can get STIs from doing this. It doesn't matter if someone is doing it or having it done to them. A person can place a barrier around the anus to prevent the spread of an STI during rimming.

Risk: Taking a chance. Having any kind of sex without a condom presents a risk for getting

STIs. Sharing drug needles can put you at risk for getting HIV and other blood borne infections including hepatitis B. Abuse of drugs and alcohol can also lead to risky behaviour.

S

Safer sex: Ways to have sexual contact that allow little to no chance of getting a sexually transmitted infection. These include properly using condoms and other barriers, mutual or self-masturbation, and abstinence from sexual contact.

Saliva: Another word for spit. It is the fluid in a person's mouth. Most STIs cannot be spread by a person's saliva.

Scrotum: The soft sac of wrinkled skin that covers and protects a man's testicles.

Selective abstinence: Someone who chooses to be selectively abstinent might have some kinds of sex but not others. Many people are sexually active but limit what they do to avoid STIs and/or pregnancy or because they do not feel ready to do some sexual things. Someone who practices selective abstinence may or may not run the risk of contracting an STI and/or having an unwanted pregnancy, depending on the activities in which he or she does.

Semen: The clear, whitish, sticky liquid that squirts out of a man's penis when he ejaculates. There are about one million sperm inside one drop of semen. Semen gives the sperm something to swim in, otherwise they couldn't move around.

Sex toys: Speciality toys that people might buy to use during sex with themselves or with another person. They could be dildos, vibrators, or other items. Sharing sex toys can be risky if they have vaginal fluids, blood, or faeces on them. Sharing sex toys without cleaning them or using a condom can potentially expose a person to STIs.

Sexual abuse: When someone mistreats another person in a sexual way. This "someone" could be someone the person knows, someone the person loves, or a stranger. Sexual abuse often involves physical contact, including forced, unwanted sexual activity such as fondling or genital contact. Not all sexual abuse involves physical contact, though.

Exposing one's genitals to another person, forcing someone to watch pornography, or pressuring someone for sex can all be forms of sexual abuse.

Sexual desire: A strong sexual interest or attraction for another person. People can have sexual desire with or without love.

Sexual fluids: The wetness that comes out of a man or a woman's genitals. For men it is semen and pre-seminal fluid and for women it is vaginal and cervical secretions. These sexual fluids transmit STIs (like HIV, chlamydia and gonorrhoea) if a person is infected.

Sexual intercourse: Any type of activity that involves the sharing of body fluids, or the penetration of an orifice (the mouth, vagina, or anus) between two or more people. Sexual intercourse also includes oral sex and anal sex. People can get STIs, including HIV, if they have sexual intercourse without a safe barrier that prevents the fluids from getting from one person to another. Other STIs, like herpes and HPV, can be transmitted during sexual intercourse, even when using a barrier, because these are transmitted through direct skin-to-skin contact.

92

Sexual orientation: Describes whether a person is homosexual, heterosexual or bisexual.

Sexual pleasure: A good feeling that people get when they engage in sexual activity with another person, or through masturbation.

Sexuality: Everything in our daily lives that makes us sexual humans. It is made up of gender, sexual desire and feelings, and sexual contact.

Sperm: A male' sex cells, tiny living things that are made in a man's testicles. When a man ejaculates, semen squirts out of his penis. This semen contains millions of sperm cells. If this happens in or near a female's vagina, the sperm can swim around and try to find an egg. If a sperm gets inside a woman's egg, she can become pregnant. Sperm can live in the vagina up to five days. If a male doesn't ejaculate then the sperm is soaked up by his own body.

Spermicide: A chemical that kills sperm, used to help prevent pregnancy. Spermicide is available as a foam, cream or jelly and can be bought at a drug store. It can be placed on the outside of a condom or inside a woman's vagina. It cannot be used by itself to stop

HIV from getting into someone else's body. Some people may be allergic to one or more chemicals in spermicide.

Sponge: Birth control that kills sperm, used as a form of contraception. A woman puts it into her vagina before vaginal sex. Sponges can help prevent pregnancy but do not protect a man or a woman from getting STIs.

Sterilization: A permanent kind of contraception. It involves a simple operation that stops egg and sperm from meeting each other. Usually older people do this when they do not want to have any more children. Sterilization can be done to a man or a woman.

Straight: Another word for heterosexual.

Symptoms: Medically speaking, a symptom is something that a person can notice about himself or herself that is a sign of a disease. Common symptoms for STIs include bumps, blisters, or warts near the genitals, a burning sensation when a person urinates, or an unusual discharge or drip from the genitals. Many people with STIs may not have any signs or symptoms. There is no sure way to tell if someone has an STI from symptoms.

Only a medical test can tell a person for sure.

T

Testicles: Two small egg-shaped male organs that hang behind the penis. They are soft and are covered and protected by the scrotum. The testicles are what make sperm.

Transfusion: Donated blood from one person given to another person when a loss of blood has occurred through surgery, an accident, or other medical needs. The donated blood supply in the U.S. is tested for HIV, hepatitis, and other types of blood diseases before it is used by others.

Transmission: The ways that any kind of infection, including an STI, can be spread. Having unprotected oral, anal, or vaginal sex, are the main ways STIs are transmitted. Blood, semen, pre-seminal fluid, vaginal and cervical secretions and breast milk are all fluids that can transmit STIs. Some STIs can also be transmitted through skin-to-skin contact.

U

Urethra: The small tube that carries urine (pee) from someone's bladder to the outside of his or her body. The opening to the urethra for a male is the hole at the tip of the penis. The opening to the urethra for a female is just above the opening to the vagina, and just below the clitoris. Germs that cause STIs can get inside someone's body through the urethra.

Urine: The liquid waste that comes out of a person's urethra when they urinate (pee).

Urethritis: An infection of the urethra, the tube that urine (pee) goes through to leave the body. Urethritis is often caused by an STI. A person with urethritis often feels a burning sensation when urinating. Urethritis can be cured with antibiotics.

Uterus: A hollow organ that is found inside the lower pelvic area of a female's body. It is connected to both of the fallopian tubes and to the vagina. This is the place where a fetus grows if a woman gets pregnant. Each month, during a part of a woman's menstrual cycle the uterus gets ready to help a baby grow by making thick walls of blood. If a woman doesn't get pregnant then this blood flows out of the body.

V

Vaccine: A mixture of killed or weakened virus or bacteria, injected into a person to help prevent disease. Since the virus or bacteria in a vaccine is either killed or weakened, the body can easily defeat it. If a person is exposed to the virus or bacteria, the body's immune system can respond, since it has already been prepared by the vaccine. There are vaccines to prevent STIs, like HPV and hepatitis B.

Vagina: The place in a female that leads from the uterus to the outside of the body. It is also called a birth canal because when a woman has a baby it comes out through here. The vagina is the place where an erect penis goes during vaginal sex. Mucous membranes line the vagina, making it easy for germs that cause STIs or other germs to get inside the body of a female. This could happen even if the penis doesn't get inside but is near the vagina.

Vaginal secretions: A clear and slippery fluid that comes from the walls of the vagina. It is a natural lubricant that comes out before and during sex. This helps the penis get inside the vagina easier and also protects the lining of the vagina and the skin on a man's penis. It is also a fluid that can give STIs to another person.

Vaginal sex: When a man puts his penis into the vagina of a woman. This can make a woman pregnant if they don't use birth control. A person can also get STIs this way if their partner is infected. Correct and consistent use of condoms can prevent pregnancy and transmission of STIs.

Virgin: A person who has never had sex. Some people think it means someone who has not had oral, anal or vaginal sex. Other people feel that a virgin is someone who has had oral sex but nothing else. The word virgin means different things to different people. Sometimes it is good to ask a boyfriend or girlfriend what they mean when they say that they are a virgin. Depending on what their definition of a virgin is, they might have already contracted a STI.

Virus: A kind of germ that can cause disease. An STI caused by a virus, like herpes, HIV, or HPV, cannot be cured, but can be treated to help make the symptoms disappear.

Vulva: The sex organs outside of a female's body. They include the labia and the clitoris.

W

Water-based lubricant: A lubricant in which the main ingredient is water. Use only water-based lubricants with latex condoms, not oil-based ones.

Wet dream: When a male has an erection and then ejaculates when sleeping. It can happen to someone without that person knowing about it. Wet dreams are perfectly normal and can happen from adolescent stage age through all stages. These are sometimes called "nocturnal emissions."

Withdrawal: When a male takes his penis out of another person's vagina, anus or mouth before ejaculation to try to stop semen from getting inside the person. This is also known as pulling out. Withdrawal is not effective at preventing pregnancy or at preventing the spread of a STI.

Womb: Another word for uterus.

Y

Yeast infection: An infection due to candida yeast. A woman can get a yeast infection in her vagina when small amounts of yeast that normally grow there go out of control. Yeast infections are treatable with medicine. Yeast can grow faster if a person takes antibiotics or birth control pills for a long time, has an allergy to yeast, or changes their diet and eats a lot of sugar.

Z

Zygote: A zygote is formed when a man's sperm fertilizes a woman's egg. It is the first step in what will later develop into an embryo, and then a fetus, and finally a baby.

References

1. Sexual Arousal and Orgasm - www.sexualityandu.ca

2. Sexual health - www.iwannaknow.org

3. The Church – Is Not What You Think – www.sbpra.com/yefulkay

4. There is a Condition – Recognising the Conditions of Successful Life

5. Life After Death – Where Would You Be If You Die Today

6. Eternity Is Just A Step Across The Threshold

7. The Downfall of Man Is Out of WWH

NOTE: references 3 to 7 were written by MAXWELL KOBINA ACQUAH (YEFULKAY)

Check out on Amazon and other online bookstores. You can also visit www.mkacquah.webs.com and www.facebook.com/mkacquah for more information.